A MACDONALD BOOK

Originally published as 'Je regarde, je comprends . . . L'eau'
by Editions des Deux Coqs d'Or, Paris

Copyright © 1987 Editions des Deux Coqs d'Or
All rights reserved

Translator and English text editor Barbara Tombs
English text consultant David Rowbotham

First published in Great Britain 1988
by Macdonald & Co (Publishers) Ltd
London & Sydney

A member of Maxwell Pergamon Publishing Corporation plc

ISBN 0 356 13962 X
      0 356 13963 8 pbk

Printed and bound by Henri Proost Turnhout, Belgium

Macdonald & Co (Publishers) Ltd
Greater London House
Hampstead Road
London NW1 7QX

British Library Cataloguing in Publication Data
Averous, Pierre
    Water. — (In the picture; 2).
    1. Water – For children
    I. Title   II. Series
    553.7

In the Picture
Water

Pierre Avérous Rosine Daëms

Macdonald

Contents

Pore over the large pictures . . . and then turn the page to discover something new. Look carefully and you'll find out more about the world we live in.

Water has many uses — page 10

Boats float on water
Water works machines
Water washes everything
Water fills reservoirs
Water comes out of taps
Water puts out fire

We can't live without water — page 14

Our bodies need water
Fish live in water
Plants are full of water
Under the microscope
Don't pollute water!
The very first animals

Following the stream — page 18

Water runs downhill
It cuts deep valleys
It polishes stones
It builds sandbanks
Water in the marshes
Water wears away caves

A walk by the sea — page 22

The sea changes beaches
Waves wear away cliffs
The wind pushes waves
Life in the sea
Farming the sea
The sea can get dirty!

The underwater world page 26

Sea-water is salty Moving seaweed
Underwater divers Mud on the sea-bed
A dark, cold world Silent creatures

Water's long journey page 30

Water evaporates When it's too cold, it snows
A mass of droplets Water from springs
Suddenly, it's raining! The first rains

Water is strange page 34

Water takes on any shape No taste or smell
Water gets you wet! Water boils easily
Water is colourless Water traps gases

Solid water! page 38

A huge sheet of ice Animals of the Poles
Icebergs on the sea Houses of snow
A frozen sea Food in the snow

Water in the desert page 42

Building sand dunes Some plants grow
Dry earth Bedouins at the oasis
Animals in the desert How to find water

Some questions and answers about water page 44

How does water turn to ice? • Why does water make our washing wet?
Why is the sea salty? • Why don't we water the deserts?
How do we clean river water? • Can we drink any spring water?
Will we ever run out of water?

Let's start off at the old water mill . . .

Water has many uses

Boats float on water

Have you ever dropped a leaf into the water and watched it? It will float, just like a little boat. Perhaps, a long time ago, that is where people got the idea of making boats. First of all they probably built canoes dug out of tree trunks, then they went on to build bigger and better boats. They found they could travel a long way carried by the water.

Water works machines

All over the world, water is used to work machines. When water runs down a steep slope, it rushes down so fast that it can turn a huge wheel round and round. This is how the water is turning the water-wheel in this picture. The water-wheel then turns the heavy millstones which crush grain to make flour. In the same way, water can turn the powerful wheels called turbines which make electricity.

Water washes everything

A face cloth, water and soap, that's all you need to have a wash, even if the soap does sting your eyes! If we didn't have water, we wouldn't be able to wash at all. We can use water to wash our dirty clothes, to rinse away the soil from vegetables, or to wash cars and railway carriages. In those countries which don't have very much water, people sometimes become ill, because it's difficult to wash and properly clean the things they use.

Water fills reservoirs

Have you ever seen a water tower? You may have seen one in the country – a tall strange-shaped tower, often at the top of a hill. Inside the tower, the water is pumped through pipes into a large tank. This water has been cleaned and filtered in a waterworks. Only then is it clean and pure enough for you to drink.

Water comes out of taps

When you turn on the tap, it seems as if the water comes out of the wall. Of course, this isn't true. Huge pipes, which are buried underground, bring water from the waterworks to towns and villages. Smaller pipes under the streets carry the water to the houses. Then it runs through the pipes in your home to the tap. The water that you use has travelled a long way from the waterworks, through many kilometres of pipes, before reaching your tap.

Water puts out fire

When you have a bonfire in the garden, you have to be sure to put it out carefully when you have finished. A good jet of water from the garden hose and it's done. On our Earth, we have air to help the fire burn, and water to put out the flames.

If you are thirsty, push open the kitchen door . . .

We can't live without water

Our bodies need water

People and animals can't live without water. Our bodies need it. Our blood, muscles and bones contain a lot of water. If people don't have enough water to drink, they can become very ill, and even die. This is why we need to drink during the day. When water travels through our body, it becomes 'dirty' and has to come out. That's when we want to do a wee.

Fish live in water

Although they live in water, fish also have to drink, just like other animals. But above all, they need the water to 'carry' them. Their bodies are made so that they can move easily. A swish of their tails moves them forward, and a flick of their fins helps them to turn easily. But did you know that frogs are also born in water? When they are born they are fish-shaped tadpoles. They only come out on to dry land when their bodies have developed enough.

Plants are full of water

When you bite into a ripe pear, you are eating and drinking at the same time, because its juice is mostly made of water. Plants take in water from the soil through their roots. It travels up through the inside of the stem, along through tiny tubes and then right to the tips of the leaves. During this journey, many products mix with the water to form what is called the sap of a plant, or to form the juice of ripe fruit.

Under the microscope

One day, a scientist had the idea of looking through a microscope at a drop of water taken from a vase of flowers. What a fabulous world the scientist discovered! Microscopic creatures were darting about in all directions. They were called microbes. They took their food from the 'used' water in the vase. In seas and rivers, there are millions of these microbes in each drop of water. They in turn are food for bigger creatures.

Don't pollute water!

We build huge factories which never stop. Every day, millions of cars use the roads. They all give out lots of smoke and gases. Some of these are very dirty and fill the air with dangerous products. Raindrops carry them back to Earth again, where they harm the plants. Other dangerous products are thrown into rivers. The whole world needs water, so we must be careful not to dirty or pollute it like this.

The very first animals

There haven't always been animals on Earth. A very long time ago there were no birds flying in the sky, and no animals on the land. There was only a very simple form of living thing with a microscopic, jelly-like body, which lived in the sea. Then, very very slowly, these creatures started to change. Eventually, some developed legs and were able to move on to the land, and today, thousands of different creatures live on land.

The canoe follows the stream . . .

Following the stream

Water runs downhill

Water streams down the slope of the roof and into the gutter. It tumbles down through rocks in a waterfall. The spring bubbles from the ground, until it becomes a stream and then flows into a river. Wherever it is, water always flows downhill towards the sea. You will never see a stream going back up a mountain, just as, if you knock over a glass of water, you will never see the water going back by itself into the glass.

It cuts deep valleys

Rivers can cut deep valleys through the countryside. As rivers flow towards the sea, they carry along pebbles and grains of sand. These twist and turn and scrape along the bottom of the river. Very, very slowly, they wear away the soil at the bottom of the river until, after thousands of years, they have cut wide, deep valleys through the countryside.

It polishes stones

Stones carried by the river roll against each other. They are pushed about by the current and bump into one another. When this happens, tiny pieces break off the stones. Gradually, they lose their sharp edges and become round and polished. After many years, each has become a smooth, round pebble. You can see pebbles like this on the beach, and it's easy to twist your ankle when you walk on them!

It builds sandbanks

As the river turns, the water travels so quickly on the outside of the bend that it gradually carves away the bank. On the inside of the bend, the water travels more slowly and leaves sand and soil behind. These eventually form a little beach, just right for pushing out a boat and going for a row. Sometimes, these beaches are found right in the middle of a wide river. We say that the water has built a sandbank.

Water in the marshes

When water comes to a hollow, it stays there. This is how lakes are formed. The lake's surface is quite still because there isn't any current moving it. We call this calm water. In other places, the land is so flat that the water doesn't seem to move. The water forms pools and channels amongst the grasses. These are called marshes, and are home to many different sorts of animals. Sometimes there are also marshes on the edges of rivers.

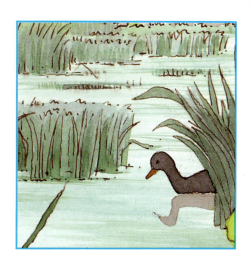

Water wears away caves

Water doesn't only flow in the open air. It can also go deep under the ground. It slips through the cracks in buried rocks. In some places, the water slowly makes these cracks bigger and bigger. Under the ground, hidden from sight, the water wears away tunnels and makes huge caves. Then one day, someone finds a hole which has opened up in the ground. They go down and discover an underground cave. In some caves you can find underground rivers too.

Come to the beach and discover the world of the sea . . .

A walk by the sea

The sea changes beaches

In large bays or in tiny coves there are beautiful beaches where you can play. These beaches are made of millions of grains of sand and pieces of shells which the sea has carried there. When there are very high tides or big storms, the sand may be carried away again. Or the sea may leave more sand. This is how the coastline slowly changes. Sometimes we have to put fresh sand on to a beach to replace what the sea has washed away.

Waves wear away cliffs

At the seaside, the waves are always pounding against the rocks. It's like being hit thousands of times by a hammer. With each blow, the rock crumbles away a little. Eventually, the waves will wear out a cave in the rock. Then one day, an enormous piece of rock crashes into the water, and the waves start attacking the rock which is left. Very slowly, cliffs are formed in this way.

The wind pushes waves

The waves crash against the bottom of the lighthouse and against the stone jetties which protect the harbour entrance. Waves look like long bumps on the surface of the sea. They are made by the wind blowing over the open sea, in much the same way that you make little waves when you blow on the soup in your spoon. When these waves come near to the beach, they roll and break in a splash of spray.

Life in the sea

Green, brown and red strips of seaweed form a wet and slippery carpet. It may look a rather strange and floppy assortment of plants, but plants they are nevertheless. The difference is they grow under the sea and at high tide they are completely covered by water. The sea is also home for many fish, sea shells, crabs and starfish. Can you find them hiding in the seaweed or in the sand?

Farming the sea

If you are by the sea in France for example, you may have noticed strange poles, covered with shellfish, called mussels. Just as we farm the land, and grow crops or keep animals, people have also decided to farm the sea. For a long time we have known how to raise oysters, and now we are learning how to watch shoals of shrimps and fish. And in China and Japan people are growing fields of seaweed.

The sea can get dirty!

The sea has so much water you'd think that it couldn't get dirty. But if an oil tanker has an accident, it may spill its load into the sea, killing thousands of sea plants and animals. The oil can harm birds which land on the sea, sticking their feathers together. The sea may also be dirtied by factories which empty out dangerous products into it. We shall have to be careful in the future if we want our seas to stay clean.

Let the divers take you under water . . .

The underwater world

Sea-water is salty

When you are swimming in the sea, try putting your head under water and opening your eyes. They sting! That's because of the salt in sea-water. A bottleful of sea-water has about a teaspoonful of salt in it. Of course, the salt doesn't worry sea creatures. They are used to it because they have always lived in the sea. Everything looks blurred under water. Divers have to wear masks to see clearly. When they look out from behind the window of their mask, they can see very well.

Underwater divers

Don't try to breathe under water – you would suffocate! Your lungs can only breathe air, not water. Underwater divers used to wear a sort of bell with portholes over their head, so that they could breathe at the bottom of the sea. A long pipe brought them air, pumped down from the surface. Today's divers take their air down with them, carrying it on their backs, packed into cylinders.

A dark, cold world

Daylight doesn't get very far under the water. Even at midday, it is dark under the waves. Everything looks bluish grey – sand, fish and seaweed. In the deepest depths there isn't any light at all. Without any warmth from the sun, the bottom of the sea is very cold. Divers have to wear special wetsuits made out of rubber to keep warm. Those who are going really deep even have to wear heated wetsuits.

Moving seaweed

Under water, the seaweed is always moving. But it can't do this by itself. It bends and sways because of the current which flows like a giant river. Even in the deepest parts of the oceans, where seaweed can't grow because it is always as dark as night, the current moves the few creatures who live there. But no diver could go that deep.

Mud on the sea-bed

Even though sea-water seems to be clear and transparent, it is full of tiny, tiny particles. You can find dust, carried by the wind or brought by currents, right in the middle of the ocean. But these particles are mostly the microscopic remains of seaweed and dead animals. They fall down slowly to the bottom of the sea and form mud, which is called sediment. Gradually, this sediment covers rocks and wrecks.

Silent creatures

We can recognize animals on land by the noise they make. But crabs, starfish or fish don't make any noise with their mouths, or very little anyway. Creatures that do are whales, which 'sing' when they want to talk to each other (although they aren't fish; they are mammals, distant relatives of cats, dogs and people!) For us water is a silent world, invaded only by the noise of boats and underwater divers.

And now let's go up into the sky . . .

Water's long journey

Water evaporates

After doing the washing, shirts, tea-towels and socks are all wet. You may hang them outside to dry them. But where does the water go to? It changes into very tiny droplets in the warmth of the Sun. These mix with the air, but they are so small it is impossible to see them. We say that the water has evaporated.

A mass of droplets

Even if you can't see it, the water which evaporates stays in the air. And there is a lot of it! Every day, a little water evaporates from all the oceans and all the rivers in the world. The leaves on trees lose water and so do animals too. In parts of the sky where it is quite cold, these invisible droplets stick to each other to form larger drops. Clouds are a huge mass of these millions of drops.

Suddenly, it's raining!

Inside the clouds, the drops are tossed about by the wind. They rise and fall, and bump into one another. They stick to one another too and get bigger and bigger. When they are too heavy to stay in the sky, they fall towards the ground: it's raining. You've just enough time to run for shelter, or to open your umbrella. . .

When it's too cold, it snows

Sometimes it's so cold that the drops of water can't stay liquid. They change into crystals of ice. Each crystal is in the shape of a star so tiny that you can only see it with a magnifying glass. These stars stick together and form magnificent snowflakes, as light as feathers. When snow falls in winter, the ground is cold enough for it not to melt when it lands. The countryside is covered with a thick, white blanket.

Water from springs

After it has rained, the earth soaks up the water like a sponge. Sometimes, water goes deep into the ground. Its underground journey may then last a long time. One day, though, the water appears again, far from the place where it went in. This usually happens where the rock is softer or where there is a crack in the rock. Where water comes out of the ground like this, we call it a spring.

The first rains

In the beginning, there was no water on our planet. It was made of rocks where nothing grew and nothing lived. Then it began to rain and it rained so much that the oceans filled up. This water came from volcanoes, which spat out huge clouds of steam. Ever since then, water has never stopped its journey between the Earth and the sky. It evaporates, forms clouds and then comes down again as rain.

Watch how light plays with water at the swimming pool . . .

Water is strange

Water takes on any shape

At the swimming pool café you can see straight glasses, round glasses, and glasses which look like funnels. When you pour water into them, the water fills them up and becomes exactly the same shape. Water is called a liquid, because it flows and instantly takes on the same shape as its container. The smallest amount of water is made of millions of microscopic ball shapes, called molecules, which roll round and crash into each other.

Water gets you wet!

What a great dive! He splashes everyone and gets them all wet! Of course that doesn't surprise you. Because we see water every day, we aren't so surprised by its marvellous qualities, but scientists have found out that other liquids do not wet things as easily, nor as well as water.

Water is colourless

When you have a bath, the water isn't any colour and you can see through it. We say that it is transparent. In the swimming pool, it looks blue because of the colour of the tiles which cover the bottom of the pool. The water in rivers is often brown or grey, because of the sand or mud in the river. In sunshine, splashes of water always seem more brilliant, because the light bounces off them.

No taste or smell

When you are thirsty, you may prefer to add fruit squash to water, because pure water, for example water which comes from a spring, doesn't generally have any taste. Sea-water has salt in it which gives it its particular taste. The water in the swimming pool, or from the tap, sometimes doesn't taste very nice, and you can smell the chlorine in it. (Chlorine is used to clean water.) But pure, clean water has no particular smell.

Water boils easily

If you want a hot drink, all you have to do is put the kettle on and then add the boiling water to tea or coffee. It's ready in five minutes! When water is heating in the kettle, the microscopic, invisible molecules dart about more and more quickly the hotter the water gets. Some even escape in the steam. When the water is bubbling furiously, the water is boiling.

Water traps gases

Lemonade is very fizzy. In the factory where it is made, gas and flavourings are added to water. As long as the bottle is kept tightly closed, the gas is invisible. But as soon as you open it, hundreds of bubbles appear. In your mouth you can taste that it's fizzy. Spring water also contains gas, but often so little that you can hardly notice it. Only a few spring waters are really fizzy.

Let's visit a land where the water is frozen solid . . .

Solid water!

A huge sheet of ice

There are vast areas on Earth where the snow never melts. It piles up and hardens to form ice. These lands are called the polar regions. They are completely covered by an enormous sheet of ice. In places, this giant glacier is more than three kilometres thick. If all this ice melted, it would turn into such an immense quantity of water that the oceans would flood.

Icebergs on the sea

The sheet of ice which covers the polar lands isn't still. It 'flows' and slides towards the sea, like a very slow river. Once it meets the sea, enormous lumps break off and drift away. These giant ice cubes are called icebergs. Those around the South Pole are quite flat. Some are so big that sailors used to think they were islands. The icebergs around the North Pole are smaller, but more jagged.

A frozen sea

Even the sea can freeze in the polar regions. In winter, it is covered with a layer of ice. This floating, frozen crust is called pack ice. Special ships, called ice breakers, have to break up the ice before it gets too thick for other ships to sail through. Ice breakers need to have very strong hulls. In the warmer summer weather, the pack ice melts again.

Animals of the Poles

In spite of the cold and the ice which invades everything, some animals live in the frozen regions of the Earth. The seals of the North Pole come up to breathe fresh air by breaking through the ice. They have to watch out for polar bears which can attack them. At the South Pole, the animals are different. You can find huge flocks of strange-looking birds, called penguins. Their wings are too small for them to fly. But they swim very well!

Houses of snow

You have probably already tried patting the snow together to make snowballs or to build a superb snowman. The Eskimos (or Inuit as they prefer to be called) who live in the frozen lands close to the North Pole can make 'bricks' of packed snow like this. A few of them still use them to build their houses, called igloos. They also melt the snow so that it becomes water when they want to drink. The Inuit use sledges to travel across the snow.

Food in the snow

In the icy world of the Arctic, some Inuit still catch seals. They eat their meat and use their fat to protect them from the cold. They make clothes with their skins. They also hunt and fish a lot. But today, many Inuit live in modern homes and buy their food and clothes from shops. No one lives at the South Pole apart from a few scientists studying nature. It is a frozen world, which is very difficult to reach from other places.

Finish your journey with a visit to the burning hot desert . . .

Water in the desert

Building sand dunes

We have seen some of the ways that water can slowly change the land. But in deserts, where there is very little water, it is the wind which does this work. It wears away rocks, blowing away the tiny pieces of sand and dust and then dropping them somewhere else. They build up to form huge sand dunes. They look like waves, although they don't seem to move. But the dunes do move – the wind is always shifting them, grain by grain.

Dry earth

It hardly ever rains in the desert. The streams are often dry. Even when it does rain, the Sun is so hot that the water soon evaporates. The puddles quickly turn into a crust of cracked earth. The bare, dry earth stretches ahead endlessly. The only things which seem to grow here are pebbles!

Animals in the desert

It's very difficult for animals to live in the desert. Those that do all have different ways of surviving. Dromedaries – camels which only have one hump – can spend several days without drinking; they live off the fat in their hump. Scorpions, spiders and centipedes hide in the shade of rocks, and lizards and snakes bury themselves in the sand. The fox doesn't come out from his den until nightfall.

Some plants grow

The leaves of date palm trees are formed in narrow pointed strips. Cacti have leaves which are completely transformed – into spikes! Desert plants often look rather dry and shrivelled up. It's so they don't lose more water than they have to through their leaves. This is how they are able to survive in the scorching Sun.

Bedouins at the oasis

For centuries, some groups of people have lived in deserts, even though there isn't much water. The Bedouins in the Sahara move on from place to place travelling with their herds of animals. They camp under the trees at the oases. In the south of Africa, the Bushmen shelter under simple huts. And the aborigines who live in the Australian outback often set up camp in the shade of a rock.

How to find water

In deserts, like everywhere else, there is water underground. But you need to know where to find it! The people who live in the desert have to dig wells, which are often very deep. For these people, because water can be so difficult to find, it is very, very precious. It means they can drink, cook, even grow some plants. Because wherever we are on our planet, none of us can live without water.

Some questions and answers about water

How does water turn to ice?

There are millions of tiny molecules in the smallest drop of water. These molecules are so small that you can't even see them through the most powerful of microscopes. When it gets very cold, each molecule 'hooks' on to its neighbour. They all hold on to each other so tightly that they can't move around as freely as before, when they were liquid water. And so you see solid water – ice. As soon as it gets warmer, the molecules let go of each other . . . and the water flows again!

Why does water make our washing wet?

Again it is because of these tiny molecules! Each molecule hangs on to the nearest thread in the material, rather like a rock climber holding on to a rock. But there are so many molecules that a single drop of water spreads out over the material and makes a large wet patch.

Why is the sea salty?

The water in streams and rivers carries along substances called mineral salts, which are found in rocks and soil. As the rivers and streams flow into lakes and eventually the seas and oceans, these mineral salts are brought to the sea, too. There they stay during millions of years. They mix with other substances during this time to slowly form the salt which gives sea-water its curious taste.

Why don't we water the deserts?

In some countries, like Israel, we do water them! But the problem is that the water evaporates too quickly. Farmers have to water the soil around lettuces and fruit trees a little at a time. Or they make small canals for the water to flow from streams directly to the plants. In this way, we can grow plants in some desert lands.

How do we clean river water?

River water is pumped to a waterworks where it is cleaned so that it's fit for us to drink. In the waterworks it goes into a large tank, where it is left undisturbed. Here all the largest pieces of dirt fall to the bottom of the tank. Then the water passes through a sort of fine grill, called filters. After it has been through the filters it *looks* very clean. But it isn't clean enough. We still have to get rid of the dangerous germs which can easily slip through the filters, because they are so small. This is done using a chemical, like chlorine. You probably know its smell from the swimming pool. Only then is the water clean enough for you to drink.

Can we drink any spring water?

No, it could be very dangerous. In the mountains, water is generally quite clean enough to drink from a spring. But as water comes down the hillsides it gets dirtier. Sometimes the chemicals which farmers use on the fields to help plants grow can get into the water, and these can be very harmful to us if we swallow them. And a lot of dirty water goes into the ground near houses. So never drink well water or water from a spring without asking a grown-up first.

Will we ever run out of water?

This has already happened in some desert lands and in some large cities. Sometimes there is not enough clean water for everyone. In many countries people are sometimes asked to save water in summer, especially when it is hot and the rivers are low. There may be a lot of water on our Earth, but it isn't always easy to get at it.

MERLEY FIRST SCHOOL
OAKLEY STRAIGHT,
WIMBORNE, DORSET BH21 1SD
TEL: (020...) ...5